Cake Mix
Cookies

Publications International, Ltd.

Favorite Brand Name Recipes at www.fbnr.com

Recipes on pages 4, 16, 30, 52, 54, 60, 62, 100, 104 and 116 developed by Maiko Miyamoto.

Recipes on pages 18, 20, 28, 36, 42, 58, 68, 72, 78, 92, 94, 98, 102, 106, 108, 110, 114, 118 and 120 developed by Alison Reich.

Photography on pages 5, 17, 19, 21, 29, 31, 37, 41, 43, 53, 55, 59, 61, 63, 69, 73, 79, 93, 95, 99, 101, 103, 105, 107, 109, 111, 115, 117, 119 and 121 by Laurie Proffitt Photography, Chicago.
Photographer: Laurie Proffitt
Photographer's Assistant: Chad Evans
Food Stylist: Carol Smoler
Assistant Food Stylist: Sheila Grannen

Pictured on the front cover: Pastel Mint Swirls *(page 86)*.
Pictured on the back cover *(top to bottom):* Toasted Coconut Cream Cheese Pinwheels *(page 28),* Easy Turtle Bars *(page 12)* and Raspberry Almond Squares *(page 62).*

ISBN-13: 978-1-4127-1674-1
ISBN-10: 1-4127-1674-8

Library of Congress Control Number: 2008934405

Manufactured in China.

8 7 6 5 4 3 2 1

Microwave Cooking: Microwave ovens vary in wattage. Use the cooking times as guidelines and check for doneness before adding more time.

Contents

Carrot Cake Cookies

1 package (about 18 ounces) spice cake mix
½ cup all-purpose flour
½ cup vegetable oil
¼ cup water
1 egg, lightly beaten
½ cup shredded carrots (about 2 medium)
½ cup walnuts, coarsely chopped
½ cup raisins
    Prepared cream cheese frosting

1. Preheat oven to 350°F. Line cookie sheets with parchment paper.

2. Combine cake mix, flour, oil, water and egg in large bowl. Stir in carrots, walnuts and raisins until well blended.

3. Drop dough by rounded tablespoonfuls 2 inches apart onto prepared cookie sheets. Bake 12 to 15 minutes or until bottoms are golden brown. Cool 1 minute on cookie sheets. Remove cookies to wire rack; cool completely.

4. Spread cookies with frosting before serving.

Makes about 3 dozen cookies

Peanut Butter Cheesecake Bars

1 package (about 18 ounces) yellow cake mix with pudding in the mix
½ cup (1 stick) butter, softened, cut into small pieces
2 packages (8 ounces each) cream cheese, softened
1 cup chunky peanut butter
3 eggs
1¼ cups sugar
1 cup salted roasted peanuts
Melted chocolate (optional)

1. Preheat oven to 325°F.

2. Beat cake mix and butter in large bowl with electric mixer at medium speed just until crumbly. Reserve 1 cup mixture in medium bowl. Press remaining dough into ungreased 13×9-inch baking pan to form crust. Bake 10 minutes; cool in pan on wire rack.

3. Beat cream cheese and peanut butter in large bowl at medium speed until fluffy. Beat in eggs, one at a time, scraping down side of bowl occasionally. Gradually beat in sugar until light and fluffy. Spoon filling over cooled crust. Combine reserved crumb mixture and peanuts; crumble over filling.

4. Bake 45 minutes or until filling is just set and knife inserted into center comes out clean. Cool 30 minutes in pan on wire rack. Refrigerate at least 2 hours before serving. Drizzle with melted chocolate, if desired.

Makes about 2 dozen bars

Blondie Biscotti with Almonds

1 cup slivered almonds
1 package (about 18 ounces) white cake mix
⅔ cup all-purpose flour
2 eggs
3 tablespoons melted butter, cooled slightly
1 teaspoon vanilla
3 tablespoons grated lemon peel

1. Preheat oven to 350°F. Line cookie sheet with parchment paper.

2. Heat medium skillet over medium heat. Add almonds and cook 1½ to 2 minutes or just until fragrant, stirring constantly. *Do not brown.* Set aside.

3. Beat cake mix, flour, eggs, butter and vanilla in large bowl with electric mixer at low speed 1 to 2 minutes or until well blended. Stir in almonds and lemon peel. Knead dough 7 to 8 times or until ingredients are well blended.

4. Divide dough in half. Shape each half into 12×2×½-inch log; place logs 3 inches apart on prepared cookie sheet.

5. Bake 25 minutes or until toothpick inserted into centers of logs comes out clean. Cool 25 minutes on cookie sheet on wire rack.

6. Trim 1 inch off ends of logs and discard. Slice logs diagonally into ½-inch slices with serrated knife. Return slices, cut sides down, to cookie sheet. Bake 10 minutes or until bottoms are golden brown. Remove to wire racks; cool completely. Store in airtight container. *Makes about 4 dozen cookies*

Pinwheel Cookies

½ cup shortening plus additional for greasing
⅓ cup plus 1 tablespoon butter, softened and divided
 2 egg yolks
½ teaspoon vanilla extract
 1 package DUNCAN HINES® Moist Deluxe® Fudge Marble Cake Mix

1. Combine ½ cup shortening, ⅓ cup butter, egg yolks and vanilla extract in large bowl. Mix at low speed with electric mixer until blended. Set aside cocoa packet from cake mix. Gradually add cake mix. Blend well.

2. Divide dough in half. Add cocoa packet and remaining 1 tablespoon butter to one half of dough. Knead until well blended and chocolate colored.

3. Roll out yellow dough between two pieces of waxed paper into 18×12×⅛-inch rectangle. Repeat with chocolate dough. Remove top pieces of waxed paper from chocolate and yellow doughs. Place yellow dough directly on top of chocolate dough. Remove remaining layers of waxed paper. Roll up jelly-roll fashion, beginning at wide side. Refrigerate 2 hours.

4. Preheat oven to 350°F. Grease baking sheets.

5. Cut dough into ⅛-inch slices. Place sliced dough 1 inch apart on prepared baking sheets. Bake at 350°F for 9 to 11 minutes or until lightly browned. Cool 5 minutes on baking sheets. Remove to cooling racks.

Makes about 3½ dozen cookies

Easy Turtle Bars

1 package (about 18 ounces) chocolate cake mix
½ cup (1 stick) butter, melted
¼ cup milk
1 cup (6 ounces) semisweet chocolate chips
1 cup chopped pecans, divided
1 jar (12 ounces) caramel ice cream topping

1. Preheat oven to 350°F. Spray 13×9-inch baking pan with nonstick cooking spray.

2. Combine cake mix, butter and milk in large bowl; stir until well blended. Spread half of mixture into prepared pan.

3. Bake 7 to 8 minutes or until edges are lightly browned. Sprinkle chocolate chips and half of pecans over partially baked crust. Drizzle with caramel topping. Drop spoonfuls of remaining batter over caramel; sprinkle with remaining pecans.

4. Bake 18 to 20 minutes or until top springs back when lightly touched. (Caramel center will be soft.) Cool completely in pan on wire rack.

Makes about 2½ dozen bars

Whoopie Pies

1 package (about 18 ounces) devil's food cake mix
1 package (4-serving size) chocolate instant pudding and pie filling mix
4 eggs
1¼ cups (2½ sticks) butter, softened, divided
1 cup water
1¼ cups marshmallow creme
¾ cup powdered sugar
½ teaspoon vanilla

1. Preheat oven to 350°F. Grease cookie sheets.

2. For cookies, beat cake mix, pudding mix, eggs, ½ cup (1 stick) butter and water in large bowl with electric mixer at low speed until just moistened. Beat at medium speed 2 minutes or until light and thick, scraping down side of bowl frequently. Drop batter by heaping tablespoonfuls 2 inches apart onto prepared cookie sheets.

3. Bake 12 to 14 minutes or until cookies spring back when lightly touched. (Cookies should be about 3 inches in diameter after baking.) Cool 5 minutes on cookie sheets. Remove to wire racks; cool completely.

4. Meanwhile, for filling, beat remaining ¾ cup (1½ sticks) butter, marshmallow creme, powdered sugar and vanilla in large bowl at high speed about 2 minutes or until light and fluffy.

5. Spread filling on flat side of half of cookies; top with remaining cookies.

Makes 2 dozen sandwich cookies

Chunky Oatmeal Raisin Cookies

1 package (about 18 ounces) yellow cake mix
1½ cup old-fashioned oats
½ cup all-purpose flour
2 teaspoon ground cinnamon
½ cup packed brown sugar
2 eggs
1 teaspoon vanilla
1 cup (2 sticks) unsalted butter, melted
1 cup raisins
1 cup walnut pieces, toasted

1. Preheat oven to 375°F. Line cookie sheets with parchment paper.

2. Combine cake mix, oats, flour and cinnamon in large bowl until well blended. Beat brown sugar, eggs and vanilla in medium bowl until well blended. Add egg mixture and melted butter to dry ingredients; stir until combined. Fold in raisins and walnuts.

3. Drop tablespoonfuls of dough 2 inches apart onto prepared cookie sheets. Bake 14 to 16 minutes or until bottoms are golden brown. Remove to wire rack; cool completely.   *Makes about 4 dozen cookies*

Tip Raisins are available in many varieties these days. In addition to the standard dark raisin, look for golden raisins and jumbo raisin blends.

Peanut Blossoms

¼ cup sugar
1 package (about 18 ounces) package yellow cake mix
1 cup peanut butter
⅓ cup butter, softened
1 egg
50 milk chocolate candy kisses, unwrapped

1. Preheat oven to 350°F. Spray cookie sheets lightly with cooking spray; set aside. Place granulated sugar in small bowl; set aside.

2. Beat cake mix, peanut butter, butter and egg in large bowl with electric mixer at medium speed until well blended. Shape dough into 1-inch balls; roll in sugar. Place 2 inches apart onto prepared cookie sheets. Press one candy into center of each ball, flattening dough slightly. Repeat with remaining dough and candies.

3. Bake 10 minutes or until edges are lightly browned. Remove cookies to wire racks; cool completely. *Makes about 4 dozen cookies*

Chocolate Chip 'n Oatmeal Cookies

1 package (18.25 or 18.5 ounces) yellow cake mix
1 cup quick-cooking rolled oats, uncooked
¾ cup (1½ sticks) butter or margarine, softened
2 eggs
1 cup HERSHEY¸S SPECIAL DARK® Chocolate Chips or HERSHEY¸S Semi-Sweet Chocolate Chips

1. Heat oven to 350°F.

2. Combine cake mix, oats, butter and eggs in large bowl; mix well. Stir in chocolate chips. Drop by rounded teaspoons onto ungreased cookie sheets.

3. Bake 10 to 12 minutes or until very lightly browned. Cool slightly; remove from cookie sheets to wire racks. Cool completely.

Makes about 4 dozen cookies

Chinese Almond Cookies

1 package (about 18 ounces) yellow cake mix
5 tablespoons butter, melted
1 egg
1½ teaspoons almond extract
30 whole almonds
1 egg yolk
1 teaspoon water

1. Beat cake mix, butter, egg and almond extract in large bowl with electric mixer at medium speed until well blended. Shape dough into ball; wrap in plastic wrap and chill 4 hours or overnight.

2. Preheat oven to 350°F. Spray cookie sheets with nonstick cooking spray; set aside.

3. Shape dough into 1-inch balls; place 2 inches apart onto prepared cookie sheets. Press 1 almond into center of each ball, flattening slightly.

4. Whisk together egg yolk and water in small bowl. Brush tops of cookies with egg yolk mixture. Bake 10 to 12 minutes or until lightly browned. Cool 5 minutes on cookie sheets. Remove to wire rack; cool completely.

Makes about 2½ dozen cookies

 Tip Almond extract has a very distinct taste that people either love or hate. If you don't like it, substitute vanilla for the almond extract.

Hermits

6 tablespoons unsalted butter, softened
¼ cup packed dark brown sugar
1 egg
1 package (about 18 ounce) yellow cake mix with pudding in the mix
⅓ cup molasses
1 teaspoon ground cinnamon
¼ teaspoon baking soda
¾ cup raisins
¾ cup chopped pecans
2½ tablespoons maple syrup
1 tablespoon unsalted butter, melted
¼ teaspoon maple flavoring
¾ cup powdered sugar

1. Preheat oven to 375°F. Line cookie sheets with parchment paper.

2. Beat butter and sugar in large bowl with electric mixer at medium-high speed until well blended. Beat in egg. Add cake mix, molasses, cinnamon and baking soda; beat just until blended. Stir in raisins and pecans. Drop batter by rounded tablespoonfuls 1½ inches apart onto prepared cookie sheets.

3. Bake 13 to 15 minutes or until set. Cool 5 minutes on cookie sheets. Remove to wire rack; cool completely.

4. Combine maple syrup, butter and maple flavoring in medium bowl. Add powdered sugar, ¼ cup at a time, stirring until smooth. Drizzle glaze over cookies. Let stand 30 minutes or until set.   *Makes about 4 dozen cookies*

Quick Peanut Butter Chocolate Chip Cookies

1 package DUNCAN HINES® Moist Deluxe® Classic Yellow Cake Mix
½ cup creamy peanut butter
½ cup butter or margarine, softened
2 eggs
1 cup milk chocolate chips

1. Preheat oven to 350°F. Grease baking sheets.

2. Combine cake mix, peanut butter, butter and eggs in large bowl. Beat at low speed with electric mixer until well blended. Stir in chocolate chips.

3. Drop by rounded teaspoonfuls onto prepared baking sheets. Bake at 350°F for 9 to 11 minutes or until lightly browned. Cool 2 minutes on baking sheets. Remove to cooling racks.   *Makes about 4 dozen cookies*

Tip: Crunchy peanut butter can be substituted for creamy peanut butter.

Snickerdoodles

3 tablespoons sugar
1 teaspoon ground cinnamon
1 package DUNCAN HINES® Moist Deluxe® Classic Yellow Cake Mix
2 eggs
¼ cup vegetable oil

1. Preheat oven to 375°F. Grease baking sheets. Place sheets of foil on counter top for cooling cookies.

2. Combine sugar and cinnamon in small bowl.

3. Combine cake mix, eggs and oil in large bowl. Stir until well blended. Shape dough into 1-inch balls. Roll in cinnamon-sugar mixture. Place balls 2 inches apart on baking sheets. Flatten balls with bottom of glass.

4. Bake at 375°F for 8 to 9 minutes or until set. Cool 1 minute on baking sheets. Remove to foil to cool completely.   *Makes about 3 dozen cookies*

Quick Peanut Butter
Chocolate Chip Cookies

Black and White Sandwich Cookies

1 package (about 18 ounces) chocolate cake mix with pudding in the mix
1½ cups (3 sticks) butter, softened, divided
2 egg yolks, divided
½ to ¾ cup milk, divided
1 package (about 18 ounces) butter recipe yellow cake mix with pudding in the mix
4 cups powdered sugar
¼ teaspoon salt

1. Preheat oven to 325°F.

2. For chocolate cookies, place half of chocolate cake mix in large bowl. Add ½ cup (1 stick) butter; beat with electric mixer at medium speed until well blended. Add 1 egg yolk and remaining cake mix; beat just until dough forms. Beat in 1 to 2 tablespoons milk if dough is too crumbly.

3. Shape dough by rounded tablespoonfuls into 36 balls. Place 2 inches apart on ungreased cookie sheets; flatten slightly. Bake 20 minutes or until cookies are set. Cool 5 minutes on cookie sheets. Remove to wire racks; cool completely.

4. For vanilla cookies, place half of yellow cake mix in large bowl. Add ½ cup (1 stick) butter; beat at medium speed until well blended. Add remaining egg yolk and cake mix; beat just until dough forms. Beat in 1 to 2 tablespoons milk if dough is too crumbly.

5. Shape dough by rounded tablespoonfuls into 36 balls. Place 2 inches apart on ungreased cookie sheets; flatten slightly. Bake 20 minutes or until cookies are set. Cool 5 minutes on cookie sheets. Remove to wire racks; cool completely.

6. Cut remaining ½ cup (1 stick) butter into small pieces. Beat butter, powdered sugar, salt and 6 tablespoons milk in large bowl with electric mixer until light and fluffy. Add additional 2 tablespoons milk, if necessary, for more spreadable frosting. Spread frosting on flat sides of chocolate cookies; top with vanilla cookies. *Makes 3 dozen sandwich cookies*

Toasted Coconut Cream Cheese Pinwheels

1¼ cups sweetened flaked coconut
1 package (about 18 ounces) white cake mix
1 (8-ounce) package cream cheese, softened
¼ cup all-purpose flour
1 teaspoon coconut extract or vanilla extract
¾ cup apricot jam

1. Preheat oven to 350°F. Spread coconut on baking sheet; bake 4 minutes. Stir coconut and bake additional 4 minutes or until lightly browned. Remove baking sheet; set aside.

2. Combine cake mix, cream cheese, flour and coconut extract in large bowl with electric mixer at low speed until well blended. Place dough between 2 sheets parchment paper and roll into rectangle about 13×10 inches. Spread jam over dough, leaving ½-inch border. Sprinkle with toasted coconut.

3. Roll dough, jelly-roll style, starting from long side. *Do not roll paper up with dough.* Wrap in plastic wrap and freeze 2 hours or refrigerate 4 to 8 hours.

4. Preheat oven to 350°F. Spray cookie sheets with cooking spray.

5. Slice dough into ¼-inch-thick slices; place 1 inch apart onto prepared cookie sheets. Bake 12 to 15 minutes or until edges are lightly browned. Cool 3 minutes on cookie sheets. Remove to wire racks; cool completely.

Makes about 3½ dozen cookies

Toasted Coconut Cream
Cheese Pinwheels

Chocolate Creations

Black Forest Bars

1 package (about 18 ounces) dark chocolate cake mix
½ cup (1 stick) unsalted butter, melted
1 egg
½ teaspoon almond extract
1¼ cup sliced almonds, divided
1 jar (about 16 ounces) maraschino cherries, well drained
½ cup semisweet chocolate chips

1. Preheat oven to 350°F. Line 13×9-inch baking pan with foil; set aside.

2. Combine cake mix, butter, egg and almond extract in large bowl with electric mixer at medium speed. Stir in ¾ cup almonds.

3. Press dough into bottom of prepared pan. Top evenly with cherries. Bake 20 to 25 minutes or until toothpick inserted into center comes out clean. Cool completely in pan on wire rack.

4. Place chocolate chips in small resealable food storage bag; seal bag. Microwave on HIGH 1 to 1½ minutes, kneading bag every 30 seconds until melted and smooth. Cut tiny corner from bag; drizzle chocolate over bars. Sprinkle with remaining ½ cup almonds. *Makes about 24 bars*

Chocolate Almond Biscotti

1 package DUNCAN HINES® Moist Deluxe® Dark Chocolate Fudge
    Cake Mix
1 cup all-purpose flour
½ cup butter or margarine, melted
 2 eggs
 1 teaspoon almond extract
½ cup chopped almonds
    White chocolate, melted (optional)

1. Preheat oven to 350°F. Line 2 baking sheets with parchment paper.

2. Combine cake mix, flour, butter, eggs and almond extract in large bowl. Beat at low speed with electric mixer until well blended; stir in almonds. Divide dough in half. Shape each half into 12×2-inch log; place logs on prepared baking sheets.

3. Bake at 350°F for 30 to 35 minutes or until toothpick inserted into centers comes out clean. Remove logs from oven; cool on baking sheets 15 minutes. Using serrated knife, cut logs into ½-inch slices. Arrange slices on baking sheets. Bake biscotti 10 minutes. Remove to cooling racks; cool completely.

4. Dip one end of each biscotti into melted white chocolate, if desired. Allow white chocolate to set at room temperature before storing biscotti in airtight container. *Makes about 2½ dozen cookies*

Chocolate Almond Biscotti

Chocolate Chip-Oat Cookies

1 package (about 18 ounces) yellow cake mix
¾ cup vegetable oil
2 eggs
1 teaspoon baking powder
1 teaspoon vanilla
1 cup uncooked old-fashioned oats
¾ cup semisweet chocolate chips

1. Preheat oven to 350°F. Lightly grease cookie sheets.

2. Beat cake mix, oil, eggs, baking powder and vanilla in large bowl with electric mixer at low speed 3 minutes or until well blended. Stir in oats and chocolate chips.

3. Drop dough by rounded tablespoonfuls 2 inches apart onto prepared cookie sheets.

4. Bake 10 minutes or until golden brown. Cool 5 minutes on cookie sheets. Remove to wire racks; cool completely.   *Makes 4 dozen cookies*

Tip Always keep cookies in an airtight container to ensure freshness.

Chocolate Chip-Oat Cookies

Espresso Glazed Walnut Bars

1 package (about 18 ounce) chocolate fudge cake mix with pudding in
the mix
5 tablespoons butter, melted
2 eggs
1 package (12 ounces) mini chocolate chips, divided
2 teaspoons espresso powder or instant coffee granules
2 cups chopped walnuts, divided

1. Preheat oven to 350°F. Line 13×9-inch pan with foil and spray lightly with cooking spray; set aside.

2. Beat cake mix, butter, eggs, half of chocolate chips and espresso powder in large bowl with electric mixer at medium speed until well blended. Stir in 1 cup walnuts. Spread batter into prepared pan and bake 25 minutes or until toothpick inserted into center comes out clean.

3. Scatter remaining chocolate chips over top. Let stand 5 minutes or until chocolate is softened. Spread chocolate in thin layer with small spatula. Sprinkle with remaining walnuts.

4. Cool completely in pan on wire rack. Drizzle with glaze.

Makes about 24 bars

Espresso Glaze: Stir together 1 cup powdered sugar, 2 teaspoons espresso powder or instant coffee granules and 1 to 2 tablespoons hot water until espresso powder has dissolved and mixture is smooth.

Chocolate Gingersnaps

¾ cup sugar
1 package (about 18 ounces) chocolate cake mix *without* pudding in the mix
⅓ cup vegetable oil
2 eggs
1 tablespoon ground ginger

1. Preheat oven to 350°F. Spray cookie sheets with nonstick cooking spray. Place sugar in shallow bowl.

2. Beat cake mix, oil, eggs and ginger in large bowl until well blended. Shape tablespoonfuls of dough into 1-inch balls; roll in sugar to coat. Place 2 inches apart onto prepared cookie sheets.

3. Bake about 10 minutes or until cookies are set. Remove to wire racks; cool completely.   *Makes about 3 dozen cookies*

Fudgy Oatmeal Butterscotch Cookies

1 package (18.25 ounces) devil's food cake mix
1½ cups quick-cooking or old-fashioned oats, uncooked
¾ cup (1½ sticks) butter, melted
2 large eggs
1 tablespoon vegetable oil
1 teaspoon vanilla extract
1¼ cups "M&M's"® Chocolate Mini Baking Bits
1 cup butterscotch chips

Preheat oven to 350°F. In large bowl combine cake mix, oats, butter, eggs, oil and vanilla until well blended. Stir in "M&M's"® Chocolate Mini Baking Bits and butterscotch chips. Drop by heaping tablespoonfuls about 2 inches apart onto ungreased cookie sheets. Bake 10 to 12 minutes. Cool 1 minute on cookie sheets. Cool completely on wire racks. Store in tightly covered container.

Makes about 3 dozen cookies

Chocolate Pecan Drops

1 (about 18 ounces) package yellow cake mix
1¼ cups pecan pieces, divided
½ cup (1 stick) butter, melted
1 cup semisweet chocolate chips, divided
2 eggs

1. Preheat oven to 350°F. Line cookie sheets with parchment paper.

2. Combine cake mix, 1 cup pecans, butter, ½ cup chocolate chips and eggs in food processor. Process until pecans are finely chopped and mixture is well blended (about 10 seconds).

3. Drop dough by rounded teaspoonfuls onto prepared cookie sheets. Bake 10 minutes or until light golden brown. Cool 2 minutes on cookie sheets. Remove to wire rack; cool completely.

4. Place remaining chocolate chips in small resealable food storage bag; seal. Microwave on HIGH 20 seconds. Gently knead bag until chips are melted and smooth. Cut tiny corner from bag; squeeze chocolate over cookies. Sprinkle with remaining pecans. *Makes about 4 dozen mini cookies*

Mint Chocolate Cookies

1 package (about 18 ounces) devil's food cake mix
5 tablespoons butter or margarine, melted
2 eggs
2 teaspoons peppermint extract, divided
1 cup semisweet chocolate chips
5 to 6 drops green food coloring
1 container (16 ounces) vanilla frosting
  Green sugar sprinkles

1. Preheat oven to 350°F. Spray cookie sheets lightly with nonstick cooking spray; set aside.

2. Beat cake mix, butter, eggs and 1 teaspoon peppermint extract in large bowl with electric mixer at medium speed 1 to 2 minutes or until blended and smooth. Stir in chocolate chips.

3. Drop by rounded tablespoonfuls 2 inches apart onto prepared cookie sheets. Bake 12 minutes or until edges are set and centers are no longer shiny. Cool 5 minutes on cookie sheet. Remove to wire rack; cool completely.

4. Stir remaining 1 teaspoon peppermint extract and food coloring into frosting. Spread 2 tablespoons frosting onto each cookie; decorate with sugar sprinkles.

Makes about 1½ dozen cookies

Triple Chocolate Cream Cheese Bars

1 package (about 18 ounces) chocolate cake mix
⅓ cup vegetable oil
3 eggs, divided
2 packages (8 ounces each) cream cheese, softened
⅓ cup sugar
1 cup sour cream
1 cup (6 ounces) semisweet chocolate chips, melted and cooled slightly
1 cup white chocolate chips

1. Preheat oven to 350°F. Grease 13×9-inch glass baking dish.

2. Combine cake mix, oil and 1 egg in medium bowl; mix well. Press into bottom of prepared baking dish. Bake 10 minutes or until set.

3. Meanwhile, beat cream cheese in large bowl with electric mixer at high speed until light and fluffy. Add remaining 2 eggs and sugar; beat until well blended. Beat in sour cream and melted chocolate until blended. Pour mixture over crust; sprinkle with white chocolate chips.

4. Bake about 50 minutes or until set. Cool completely in pan on wire rack. Refrigerate until serving. *Makes about 18 bars*

Triple Chocolate Cream Cheese Bar

Chocolate Hazelnut Cookies

½ cup chopped pecans
1 package (8 ounces) cream cheese, softened
½ cup (1 stick) butter, softened
1 egg
1 package (about 18 ounces) devil's food cake mix
1 jar (12 ounces) chocolate hazelnut spread
¼ cup powdered sugar

1. Preheat oven 350°F.

2. Place pecans in small resealable food storage bag. Finely crush pecans with meat mallet or rolling pin. Place in small skillet over medium-high heat; cook and stir 1½ minutes or until browned. Remove from heat and set aside.

3. Beat cream cheese and butter in medium bowl with electric mixer at low speed 30 seconds or until smooth. Add egg; beat at medium speed until well blended. Add cake mix; beat at low speed 2 minutes or until mixture is smooth. Stir in pecans. Shape dough into 1-inch balls. Spray palms lightly with nonstick cooking spray, if necessary, to make handling easier. Place 1 inch apart on ungreased cookie sheets.

4. Bake 8 minutes. (Cookies will appear undercooked.) Cool 5 minutes on cookie sheets. Remove to wire racks; cool completely.

5. Spoon 1 teaspoon chocolate hazelnut spread on top of each cookie; sprinkle with powdered sugar.

Makes 4 dozen cookies

Chocolate and Oat Toffee Bars

¾ cup (1½ sticks) plus 2 tablespoons butter, softened, divided
1 package (about 18 ounces) yellow cake mix with pudding in the mix
2 cups uncooked old-fashioned oats
¼ cup packed brown sugar
1 egg
½ teaspoon vanilla
1 cup toffee baking bits
½ cup chopped pecans
⅓ cup semisweet chocolate chips

1. Preheat oven to 350°F. Grease 13×9-inch baking pan.

2. Beat ¾ cup (1½ sticks) butter in large bowl with electric mixer at medium speed until creamy. Add cake mix, oats, brown sugar, egg and vanilla; beat 1 minute or until well blended. Stir in toffee bits and pecans. Spread dough into prepared pan.

3. Bake 30 to 35 minutes or until golden brown. Cool completely in pan on wire rack.

4. Melt remaining 2 tablespoons butter and chocolate chips in small saucepan over low heat. Drizzle warm glaze over bars. Let stand at room temperature 1 hour or until glaze is set. *Makes about 30 bars*

Cappuccino Cookies

1 package (about 18 ounces) devil's food cake mix
¾ cup milk
8 egg whites
1 tablespoon instant coffee granules
1 teaspoon ground cinnamon

1. Preheat oven to 400°F. Lightly spray cookie sheets with nonstick cooking spray.

2. Mix cake mix, milk, egg whites, instant coffee and cinnamon in medium bowl with spatula until well blended. Drop dough by rounded teaspoonfuls onto prepared cookie sheets.

3. Bake 5 minutes or until centers are set. Cool 1 minute on cookie sheets. Remove to wire racks; cool completely.   *Makes about 4 dozen cookies*

Tip Instant coffee and instant espresso are great to have on hand. Adding a small amount will intensify the chocolatey flavor in baked goods.

Pistachio Biscotti

1 package (about 18 ounces) devil's food cake mix
1 cup all-purpose flour
½ cup shelled pistachio nuts, coarsely chopped
½ cup butter (1 stick), melted
2 eggs, lightly beaten
½ cup milk or white chocolate chips

1. Preheat oven to 350°F. Line cookie sheet with parchment paper.

2. Combine cake mix and flour in medium bowl with electric mixer at low speed until blended. Beat in pistachios, butter and eggs at medium speed until combined.

3. Shape dough on prepared cookie sheet into 2 (9×5-inch) rectangles, slightly mounding in center.

4. Bake 30 to 35 minutes or until toothpick inserted into center comes out clean. Remove cookie sheet from oven; cool 15 minutes.

5. Trim 1 inch off each end of rectangle and discard. Slice each rectangle diagonally into 12 (1-inch thick) pieces. Return slices to cookie sheet; bake 10 minutes. *Turn off oven.* Let stand in oven for 30 to 40 minutes or until biscotti are crisp. Cool completely on wire rack.

6. Place chocolate chips in small resealable food storage bag. Microwave on HIGH 30 seconds. Repeat if necessary. Snip small tip of corner of bag; drizzle chocolate over biscotti.   *Makes 2 dozen cookies*

Fun and Fruity

Coconut Key Lime Bars

1 package (about 18 ounces) white cake mix
1 cup toasted coconut, plus additional for garnish
½ cup (1 stick) butter, melted
1 can (14 ounces) sweetened condensed milk
1 package (8 ounces) cream cheese, softened
  Grated peel and juice of 3 limes
3 eggs

1. Preheat oven to 350°F. Line 13×9-inch pan with foil, leaving 2-inch overhang on sides.

2. Combine cake mix, 1 cup coconut and butter in large bowl; mix until crumbly. Press mixture into bottom of prepared pan. Bake 12 minutes or until light golden brown.

3. Beat sweetened condensed milk, cream cheese, lime peel and juice in another large bowl with electric mixer at medium speed 2 minutes or until well blended; scrape down sides of bowl. Beat in eggs one at a time. Spread mixture evenly over crust.

4. Bake for 20 minutes or until filling is set and edges are lightly browned. Sprinkle with toasted coconut. Cool completely in pan on wire rack.

Makes about 24 bars

Chocolate Cherry Cookies

  1 package (8 ounces) chocolate cake mix
  3 tablespoons milk
  ½ teaspoon almond extract
10 maraschino cherries, rinsed, drained and cut into halves
  2 tablespoons white chocolate chips
  ½ teaspoon canola oil

1. Preheat oven to 350°F. Spray cookie sheets with nonstick cooking spray.

2. Beat cake mix, milk and almond extract in medium bowl with electric mixer at low speed. Increase speed to medium when mixture looks crumbly; beat 2 minutes or until smooth dough forms. (Dough will be very sticky.)

3. Coat hands with cooking spray. Shape dough into 1-inch balls. Place balls 2½ inches apart onto prepared cookie sheets; flatten slightly. Place cherry half in center of each cookie.

4. Bake 8 to 9 minutes or until cookies are no longer shiny and tops begin to crack. Remove to wire racks; cool completely.

5. Place white chocolate chips and oil in small microwavable bowl. Microwave on HIGH 30 seconds; stir. Repeat as necessary until chips are melted and mixture is smooth. Drizzle white chocolate mixture over cookies. Let stand until set.

Makes about 2 dozen cookies

Cobbled Fruit Bars

1½ cups apple juice
  1 cup (6 ounces) chopped dried apricots
  1 cup (6 ounces) raisins
  1 package (6 ounces) dried cherries
  1 teaspoon cornstarch
  1 teaspoon ground cinnamon
  1 package (about 18 ounces) yellow cake mix
  2 cups old-fashioned oats
  ¾ cup (1½ sticks) butter, melted
  1 egg

1. Combine apple juice, apricots, raisins, cherries, cornstarch and cinnamon in medium saucepan, stirring until cornstarch is dissolved. Bring to a boil over medium heat. Boil 5 minutes, stirring constantly. Remove from heat; cool to room temperature.

2. Preheat oven to 350°F. Line 15×10-inch jelly-roll pan with foil and spray lightly with cooking spray; set aside.

3. Combine cake mix and oats in large bowl; stir in butter. (Mixture may be dry and clumpy.) Add egg; stir until well blended.

4. With damp hands, press three-fourths mixture into prepared pan. Spread fruit evenly over top. Sprinkle remaining dough mixture over fruit. Bake 25 to 30 minutes or until edges and top are lightly browned. Cool completely in pan on wire rack.   *Makes about 36 bars*

Citrus Coolers

1½ cups powdered sugar
1 package (about 18 ounces) lemon cake mix
1 cup (4 ounces) pecan pieces
½ cup all-purpose flour
½ cup (1 stick) butter, melted
Grated peel and juice of 1 large orange

1. Preheat oven to 375°F. Line cookie sheets with parchment paper. Place powdered sugar in medium bowl; set aside.

2. Combine cake mix, pecans, flour, butter, orange peel and juice in large bowl with electric mixer at medium speed until well blended. Drop tablespoonfuls of dough 2 inches apart onto prepared cookie sheets.

3. Bake 13 to 15 minutes or until bottoms are light golden brown. Cool 3 minutes on cookie sheets; roll in powdered sugar. Remove to wire rack; cool completely. *Makes about 4½ dozen cookies*

Tip To quickly make pecan pieces out of whole pecans, place 4 ounces of pecans in a food processor. Process about 5 seconds or until roughly chopped.

Raspberry Almond Squares

1 package (about 18 ounces) yellow cake mix
½ cup sliced almonds, coarsely chopped
½ cup (1 stick) butter, melted
1 jar (12 ounces) seedless raspberry jam
1 package (8 ounces) cream cheese, softened
2 tablespoons all-purpose flour
1 egg

1. Preheat oven to 350°F. Line 13×9 baking pan with foil.

2. Beat cake mix, almonds and butter in large bowl with electric mixer at medium speed until crumbly. Reserve 1 cup mixture; press remaining mixture into bottom of prepared pan. Bake 10 to 12 minutes or until light golden brown.

3. Spread jam evenly over baked crust. Beat cream cheese, flour and egg in medium bowl at medium speed until combined. Spread gently over jam; top with reserved crumb mixture.

4. Bake 18 to 20 minutes or until top is light golden brown. Cool completely in pan on wire rack.   *Makes about 24 bars*

Tip: When lining pan with foil, allow 2 inches to hang over each end. Once the bars cool, you will be able to lift out the entire pan with ease.

Creamy Lemon Bars

1 package (2-layer size) lemon cake mix
3 large eggs, divided
½ cup oil
2 packages (8 ounces each) PHILADELPHIA® Cream Cheese, softened
1 container (8 ounces) BREAKSTONE'S® or KNUDSEN® Sour Cream
½ cup granulated sugar
1 teaspoon grated lemon peel
1 tablespoon lemon juice
Powdered sugar

MIX cake mix, 1 of the eggs and oil. Press mixture onto bottom and up sides of lightly greased 15×10×1-inch baking pan. Bake at 350°F for 10 minutes.

MIX cream cheese with electric mixer on medium speed until smooth. Add remaining 2 eggs, sour cream, granulated sugar, lemon peel and juice; mix until blended. Pour batter into crust.

BAKE at 350°F for 30 to 35 minutes or until filling is just set in center and edges are light golden brown. Cool. Sprinkle with powdered sugar. Cut into bars.

Makes 2 dozen bars

Storage Know-How: Store leftover bars in tightly covered container in refrigerator.

Cranberry Gems

⅔ cup dried cranberries or dried cherries
½ cup granulated sugar
3 tablespoons water, divided
1 package (about 18 ounces) white cake mix with pudding in the mix
2 eggs
2 tablespoons vegetable oil
¼ teaspoon almond extract or vanilla
½ cup powdered sugar
1 to 2 teaspoons milk

1. Preheat oven to 350°F. Lightly grease cookie sheets.

2. Combine cranberries, granulated sugar and 1 tablespoon water in small microwavable bowl. Microwave on HIGH 1 minute. Let cranberries stand 10 minutes; drain.

3. Blend cake mix, eggs, remaining 2 tablespoons water, oil and almond extract in large bowl until smooth. Drop dough by rounded teaspoonfuls 2 inches apart onto prepared cookie sheets. Top cookies with several cranberries.

4. Bake 10 minutes or until edges are lightly browned. Top cookies with 1 to 2 additional cranberries after baking. Remove to wire racks; cool completely.

5. Blend powdered sugar and 1 teaspoon milk in small bowl until smooth. Add additional 1 teaspoon milk, if necessary, to reach drizzling consistency. Drizzle glaze over cookies with tip of small spoon or fork.

Makes about 5 dozen cookies

Trail Mix Breakfast Bars

1 package (about 18 ounce) package spice cake mix with pudding in the mix
½ cup old-fashioned oats
½ cup (1 stick) butter or margarine, melted
2 eggs
2 tablespoons packed brown sugar
2 packages (6 ounces each) trail mix *or* ⅔ cup *each* candy-coated chocolate pieces, chopped nuts and raisins

1. Preheat oven to 350°F. Line 13×9-inch baking pan with foil and spray lightly with cooking spray; set aside.

2. Beat cake mix, oats, butter, eggs and brown sugar in large bowl with electric mixer at medium speed until well blended (batter will be stiff). Stir in trail mix.

3. With damp hands, press mixture into prepared pan. Bake 25 minutes or until edges are lightly browned. Cool completely in pan on wire rack. Loosen foil and slide onto cutting board; cut into bars. Store leftovers in airtight container.

Makes about 18 bars

Apricot Drops

1 package (about 18 ounces) yellow cake mix with pudding in the mix
½ cup all-purpose flour
½ cup vegetable oil
2 eggs
1 cup chopped dried apricots

1. Preheat oven to 350°F. Grease cookie sheets.

2. Beat cake mix, flour, oil and eggs in large bowl with electric mixer at medium speed 3 to 4 minutes or until well blended. Stir in apricots.

3. Drop dough by teaspoonfuls onto prepared cookie sheets. Bake 8 to 10 minutes or until golden brown. Cool 1 minute on cookie sheets. Remove to wire racks; cool completely.

Makes about 3 dozen cookies

Banana Gingerbread Bars

1 package (14.5 ounces) gingerbread cake mix
½ cup lukewarm water
1 ripe, medium DOLE® Banana, mashed (about ½ cup)
1 egg
1 small DOLE® Banana, peeled and chopped
½ cup DOLE® Seedless Raisins
½ cup slivered almonds
1½ cups powdered sugar
    Juice from 1 lemon

• Preheat oven to 350°F.

• In large mixer bowl, combine gingerbread mix, water, mashed banana and egg. Beat on low speed of electric mixer 1 minute.

• Stir in chopped banana, raisins and almonds.

• Spread batter in greased 13×9-inch baking pan. Bake 20 to 25 minutes or until top springs back when lightly touched.

• In medium bowl, mix powdered sugar and 3 tablespoons lemon juice to make thin glaze. Spread over warm gingerbread. Cool before cutting into bars. Sprinkle with additional powdered sugar, if desired.   *Makes about 32 bars*

Lemon Crumb Bars

1 (18.25- or 18.5-ounce) package lemon or yellow cake mix
½ cup (1 stick) butter or margarine, softened
1 egg
2 cups finely crushed saltine crackers
1 (14-ounce) can EAGLE BRAND® Sweetened Condensed Milk
    (NOT evaporated milk)
½ cup lemon juice
3 egg yolks

1. Preheat oven to 350°F. In large bowl, combine cake mix, butter and 1 egg with mixer until crumbly. Stir in cracker crumbs. Reserve 2 cups crumb mixture. Press remaining crumb mixture firmly on bottom of greased 13×9-inch baking pan. Bake 15 to 20 minutes or until golden.

2. With mixer or wire whisk, beat EAGLE BRAND®, lemon juice and 3 egg yolks. Spread evenly over prepared crust. Top with reserved crumb mixture.

3. Bake 20 minutes longer or until set and top is golden. Cool. Cut into bars. Store leftovers covered in refrigerator.   *Makes 2 to 3 dozen bars*

Orange Coconut Cream Bars

1 (18¼-ounce) package yellow cake mix
1 cup quick-cooking or old-fashioned oats, uncooked
¾ cup chopped nuts
½ cup butter or margarine, melted
1 large egg
1 (14-ounce) can sweetened condensed milk
2 teaspoons grated orange zest
1 cup shredded coconut
1 cup "M&M's"® Semi-Sweet Chocolate Mini Baking Bits

Preheat oven to 375°F. Lightly grease 13×9×2-inch baking pan; set aside. In large bowl combine cake mix, oats, nuts, butter and egg until ingredients are thoroughly moistened and mixture resembles coarse crumbs. Reserve 1 cup mixture. Firmly press remaining mixture onto bottom of prepared pan; bake 10 minutes. In separate bowl combine condensed milk and orange zest; spread over baked base. Combine reserved crumb mixture, coconut and "M&M's"® Semi-Sweet Chocolate Mini Baking Bits; sprinkle evenly over condensed milk mixture and press in lightly. Continue baking 20 to 25 minutes or until golden brown. Cool completely. Cut into bars. Store in tightly covered container.
Makes 26 bars

Apricot Shortbread Diamonds

1 package (about 18 ounces) yellow cake mix
2 eggs
¼ cup vegetable oil
1 tablespoon water
1 cup apricot jam or orange marmalade
1 cup (about 6 ounces) diced dried apricots
1 cup sliced almonds

1. Preheat oven to 350°F. Line 15×10-inch jelly-roll pan with foil and spray lightly with cooking spray; set aside.

2. Combine cake mix, eggs, oil and water in large bowl with electric mixer at medium speed until well blended. With damp hands, press dough into prepared pan.

3. Place marmalade in small microwavable bowl. Heat on HIGH 20 seconds to soften. Spread marmalade evenly over dough; sprinkle apricots and almonds over top.

4. Bake 25 minutes or until edges are browned and marmalade bubbles at edges. Cool completely in pan on wire rack. To cut cookies into diamonds, cut crosswise at 2-inch intervals, then cut diagonally at 2-inch intervals.

Makes 36 bars

Buried Cherry Bars

1 jar (10 ounces) maraschino cherries
1 package (about 18 ounces) devil's food cake mix
1 cup (2 sticks) butter, melted
1 egg
½ teaspoon almond extract
1½ cups semisweet chocolate chips
¾ cup sweetened condensed milk
½ cup chopped pecans

1. Preheat oven to 350°F. Lightly grease 13×9-inch baking pan. Drain cherries, reserving 2 tablespoons juice. Cut cherries into quarters.

2. Combine cake mix, butter, egg and almond extract in large bowl; blend well. (Batter will be very thick.) Stir in cherries. Spread batter in prepared pan.

3. Combine chocolate chips and sweetened condensed milk in small saucepan. Cook and stir over low heat until chocolate melts. Stir in reserved cherry juice. Spread chocolate mixture over cherries in pan; sprinkle with pecans.

4. Bake 35 minutes or until center is firm to the touch. Cool completely in pan on wire rack. *Makes about 2 dozen bars*

Quick Fruit & Lemon Drops

½ cup sugar
1 package (about 18 ounces) lemon cake mix
⅓ cup water
¼ cup (½ stick) butter, softened
1 egg
1 tablespoon grated lemon peel
1 cup mixed dried fruit bits

1. Preheat oven to 350°F. Grease cookie sheets. Place sugar in shallow bowl.

2. Beat cake mix, water, butter, egg and lemon peel in large bowl with electric mixer at low speed until well blended. Beat in fruit bits just until blended. Shape dough by heaping tablespoonfuls into balls; roll in sugar to coat. Place 2 inches apart onto prepared cookie sheets.

3. Bake 12 to 14 minutes or until set. Cool 2 minutes on cookie sheets. Remove to wire racks; cool completely. *Makes about 2 dozen cookies*

Note: If dough is too sticky to handle, add about ¼ cup all-purpose flour.

Tip Add about 1 teaspoon of grated lemon peel to dipping sugar for even more lemon flavor.

Just for Kids

PB&J Cookie Bars

1 package (about 18 ounce) yellow cake mix with pudding in the mix
1 cup peanut butter
½ cup vegetable oil
2 eggs
1 jar (12 ounces) strawberry jam
1 cup peanut butter chips

1. Preheat oven to 350°F. Line 15×10-inch jelly-roll pan with foil and spray lightly with cooking spray; set aside.

2. Beat cake mix, peanut butter, oil and eggs in large bowl with electric mixer at medium speed until well blended. With damp hands, press mixture evenly into prepared pan. Bake 20 minutes; remove from oven.

3. Place jam in small microwavable bowl; heat on HIGH 20 seconds to soften. Spread jam evenly over cookie base. Scatter peanut butter chips over top.

4. Bake 10 minutes or until edges are browned. Cool completely in pan on wire rack.   *Makes about 36 bars*

Sunshine Sandwiches

⅓ cup coarse or granulated sugar
¾ cup (1½ sticks) plus 2 tablespoons butter, softened and divided
1 egg
2 tablespoons grated lemon peel
1 package (about 18 ounces) lemon cake mix with pudding in the mix
¼ cup yellow cornmeal
2 cups sifted powdered sugar
2 to 3 tablespoons lemon juice

1. Preheat oven to 375°F. Place coarse sugar in shallow bowl.

2. Beat ¾ cup butter in large bowl with electric mixer at medium speed until fluffy. Add egg and lemon peel; beat 30 seconds. Add cake mix, one third at a time, beating at low speed after each addition until blended. Stir in cornmeal. (Dough will be stiff.)

3. Shape dough into 1-inch balls; roll in coarse sugar to coat. Place 2 inches apart on ungreased cookie sheets. Bake 8 to 9 minutes or until edges are lightly browned. Cool 1 minute on cookie sheets. Remove to wire racks; cool completely.

4. Meanwhile, beat powdered sugar and remaining 2 tablespoons butter in small bowl with electric mixer at low speed until blended. Gradually add enough lemon juice to reach spreading consistency.

5. Spread 1 slightly rounded teaspoon frosting on flat side of one cookie; top with second cookie. Repeat with remaining frosting and cookies. Store covered at room temperature for up to 24 hours or freeze up to 3 months.

Makes 2½ dozen sandwich cookies

Chocolate Peanut Butter Candy Bars

1 package (about 18 ounces) devil's food or dark chocolate cake mix
1 can (5 ounces) evaporated milk
⅓ cup butter, melted
½ cup dry-roasted peanuts
4 packages (1½ ounces each) chocolate peanut butter cups, coarsely
   chopped

1. Preheat oven to 350°F. Lightly grease 13×9-inch baking pan.

2. Beat cake mix, evaporated milk and butter in large bowl with electric mixer at medium speed until well blended. (Dough will be stiff.) Spread two thirds of dough in prepared pan. Sprinkle with peanuts.

3. Bake 10 minutes; remove from oven and sprinkle with chopped candy.

4. Drop remaining dough by large tablespoonfuls over candy. Bake 15 to 20 minutes or until center is firm to the touch. Cool completely in pan on wire rack.   *Makes about 24 bars*

Tip Devil's food is a term for something chocolatey, dense and rich. It is the opposite of angel food which is light and airy.

Cinnamon Cereal Crispies

½ cup sugar
2 teaspoons ground cinnamon, divided
1 package (about 18 ounces) white or yellow cake mix with pudding
    in the mix
½ cup water
⅓ cup vegetable oil
1 egg
2 cups crisp rice cereal
1 cup cornflakes
1 cup raisins
1 cup chopped nuts (optional)

1. Preheat oven to 350°F. Lightly spray cookie sheets with nonstick cooking spray. Combine sugar and 1 teaspoon cinnamon in small bowl.

2. Beat cake mix, water, oil, egg and remaining 1 teaspoon cinnamon in large bowl with electric mixer at medium speed 1 minute. Gently stir in rice cereal, cornflakes, raisins and nuts, if desired, until well blended. Drop dough by rounded tablespoonfuls 2 inches apart onto prepared cookie sheets. Sprinkle with half of cinnamon-sugar.

3. Bake about 15 minutes or until lightly browned. Sprinkle cookies with remaining cinnamon-sugar. Remove to wire racks; cool completely.

Makes about 5 dozen cookies

Pastel Mint Swirls

⅓ cup coarse or granulated sugar
1 package (about 18 ounces) devil's food cake mix
3 eggs
¼ cup unsweetened cocoa powder
¼ cup (½ stick) butter, melted
1½ cups small pastel mint chips

1. Preheat oven to 375°F. Place sugar in shallow bowl.

2. Combine cake mix, eggs, cocoa and butter in large bowl just until blended.
(Dough will be stiff.)

3. Shape dough into 1-inch balls; roll in sugar to coat. Place 2 inches apart on
ungreased cookie sheets.

4. Bake 8 to 9 minutes or until tops are cracked. Gently press 3 chips into top
of each cookie. Cool 1 minute on cookie sheets. Remove to wire racks; cool
completely.   *Makes 4 dozen cookies*

Jam Jam Bars

1 package (about 18 ounces) yellow cake mix with pudding in the mix
½ cup (1 stick) butter, melted
1 cup raspberry jam or apricot preserves
1 package (6 ounces) milk chocolate and peanut butter chips

1. Preheat oven to 350°F. Lightly spray 13×9-inch baking pan with nonstick cooking spray.

2. Combine cake mix and melted butter in large bowl until well blended. Reserve ½ cup dough in medium bowl; set aside. Press remaining dough evenly into prepared pan. Spread jam evenly over dough.

3. Stir milk chocolate and peanut butter chips into reserved dough until well blended. Sprinkle mixture evenly over jam.

4. Bake 20 minutes or until lightly browned and bubbly. Cool completely in pan on wire rack. *Makes 24 bars*

Sweet Mysteries

1 package (about 18 ounces) yellow cake mix with pudding in the mix
½ cup (1 stick) butter, softened
1 egg yolk
1 cup ground pecans
36 milk chocolate candy kisses, unwrapped
Powdered sugar

1. Preheat oven to 300°F. Beat half of cake mix and butter in large bowl with electric mixer at high speed until blended. Add egg yolk and remaining cake mix; beat at medium speed just until dough forms. Stir in pecans.

2. Shape rounded tablespoonfuls dough around each candy kiss, making sure candy is completely covered. Place 1 inch apart on ungreased cookie sheets.

3. Bake 20 to 25 minutes or until firm and golden brown. Cool 10 minutes on cookie sheets. Place waxed paper under wire racks. Remove cookies to wire racks; dust with powdered sugar. *Makes 3 dozen cookies*

Garbage Pail Cookies

1 package (about 18 ounces) white cake mix with pudding in the mix
½ cup (1 stick) butter, softened
2 eggs
1 teaspoon ground cinnamon
1 teaspoon vanilla
½ cup peanut butter chips
½ cup salted peanuts
½ cup mini candy-coated chocolate pieces
1½ cups crushed salted potato chips

1. Preheat oven to 350°F. Lightly grease cookie sheets.

2. Beat cake mix, butter, eggs, cinnamon and vanilla in large bowl with electric mixer at medium speed 2 minutes or until well blended. Stir in peanut butter chips, peanuts and candy-coated chocolate pieces. Stir in potato chips. (Dough will be stiff.) Drop batter by rounded tablespoonfuls 2 inches apart onto prepared cookie sheets.

3. Bake 15 minutes or until golden brown. Cool 2 minutes on cookie sheets. Remove to wire racks; cool completely.   *Makes about 3 dozen cookies*

Nutty S'mores Bars

Crust
2¼ cups graham cracker crumbs (14 whole graham crackers, crushed)
½ cup (1 stick) butter, melted
3 tablespoons sugar

Batter
1 package (about 18 ounces) milk chocolate cake mix with pudding in the mix
½ cup (1 stick) butter, melted
⅓ cup water
1 egg
½ cup mini semisweet chocolate chips

Topping
4 whole graham crackers, chopped into ½-inch pieces
1 cup mini marshmallows
1 cup roasted salted peanuts
1 cup mini semisweet chocolate chips

1. Preheat oven to 350°F. Line 13×9-inch baking pan with foil and spray lightly with cooking spray; set aside.

2. For crust, combine crumbs, butter and sugar in medium bowl until well blended. Press crumb mixture into prepared pan. Bake 10 minutes; set aside.

3. For batter, combine cake mix, butter, water and egg in large bowl with electric mixer at low speed 1 minute or until well blended. Stir in chocolate chips (batter will be stiff). Spread gently over crust in even layer. Bake 25 minutes or until toothpick inserted into center comes out clean.

4. For topping, adjust broiler rack and preheat broiler. Sprinkle chopped graham crackers, marshmallows, peanuts and chocolate chips over bars. Broil 2 to 3 minutes or until marshmallows puff and are lightly browned.

5. Cool completely in pan on wire rack. Remove bars to cutting board; cut into squares to serve. *Makes about 24 bars*

Cinnamon-Sugar Knots

¼ cup granulated sugar
¾ teaspoon ground cinnamon
1 package (about 18 ounces) spice cake mix
1 package (8 ounces) cream cheese, softened

1. Preheat oven to 350°F. Combine sugar and cinnamon in small bowl.

2. Beat cake mix and cream cheese together in large bowl with electric mixer at medium speed until well blended.

3. Shape dough into 1-inch balls; roll each ball into log about 4 inches long. Gently coil dough and pull up ends to form "knot". Place about 1½ inches apart on ungreased cookie sheets. Sprinkle with cinnamon-sugar. Bake 10 to 12 minutes or until edges are lightly browned.

4. Cool 2 minutes on cookie sheets. Remove to wire racks. Serve warm or cool completely before serving. *Makes about 4 dozen cookies*

Tip
If making the knots seems like too much work, these cookies are also delicious when baked as simple 1-inch balls.

Cinnamon-Sugar Knots

Ooey-Gooey Caramel Peanut Butter Bars

1 package (about 18 ounces) yellow cake mix
1 cup uncooked old-fashioned oats
⅔ cup creamy peanut butter
1 egg, slightly beaten
2 tablespoons milk
1 package (8 ounces) cream cheese, softened
1 jar (about 12 ounces) caramel ice cream topping
1 cup semisweet chocolate chips

1. Preheat oven to 350°F. Lightly grease 13×9-inch baking pan.

2. Combine cake mix and oats in large bowl. Cut in peanut butter with pastry blender or two knives until mixture is crumbly.

3. Blend egg and milk in small bowl. Add to peanut butter mixture; stir just until combined. Reserve 1½ cups mixture. Press remaining peanut butter mixture into prepared pan.

4. Beat cream cheese in small bowl with electric mixer at medium speed until fluffy. Add caramel topping; beat just until combined. Carefully spread over peanut butter layer in pan. Break up reserved peanut butter mixture into small pieces; sprinkle over cream cheese layer. Sprinkle with chocolate chips.

5. Bake 30 minutes or until nearly set in center. Cool completely in pan on wire rack. *Makes about 24 bars*

Ooey-Gooey Caramel
Peanut Butter Bars

Spiky Pretzel Balls

2 cups slightly crushed, thin pretzel sticks
1 package (about 18 ounces) carrot or spice cake mix
5 tablespoons butter or margarine, melted
2 eggs
1 cup chow mein noodles
1 cup mini semisweet chocolate chips
1 cup butterscotch or peanut butter chips

1. Preheat oven to 350°F. Spray cookie sheets lightly with cooking spray. Place pretzels in shallow bowl.

2. Combine cake mix, butter and eggs in large bowl until well blended. Stir in chow mein noodles, chocolate chips and butterscotch chips. Shape dough into 1-inch balls; roll in pretzel pieces, pressing firmly to adhere.

3. Place 1 inch apart onto prepared cookie sheets. Bake 14 minutes or until dough is no longer shiny. Cool 5 minutes on cookie sheets. Remove to wire racks; cool completely. Store leftovers in airtight container.

Makes about 3 dozen cookies

Coconut Clouds

1 package (about 16 ounces) confetti angel food cake mix
½ cup water
1½ cups sweetened flaked coconut
1¼ cup slivered almonds, divided

1. Preheat oven to 325°F. Line cookie sheets with parchment paper; set aside.

2. Beat cake mix and water in large bowl with electric mixer at medium-high speed 3 minutes or until fluffy. Add coconut and 1 cup almonds; beat until combined. Drop tablespoonfuls dough 2 inches apart onto prepared cookie sheets. Sprinkle tops with remaining ¼ cup almonds.

3. Bake 18 to 20 minutes or until bottoms are golden brown. Cool 1 minute on cookie sheets. Remove to wire rack; cool completely.

Makes about 4 dozen cookies

Moon Rocks

1 package (about 18 ounces) devil's food or German chocolate cake mix with pudding in the mix
3 eggs
½ cup (1 stick) butter, melted
2 cups slightly crushed (2½-inch) pretzel sticks
1½ cups uncooked old-fashioned oats
1 cup swirled chocolate and white chocolate chips or candy-coated semisweet chocolate baking pieces

1. Preheat oven to 350°F.

2. Combine cake mix, eggs and butter in large bowl; mix well. Stir in pretzels, oats and chocolate chips. (Dough will be stiff.) Drop dough by rounded tablespoonfuls 2 inches apart onto ungreased cookie sheets.

3. Bake 7 to 9 minutes or until set. Cool 1 minute on cookie sheets. Remove to wire racks; cool completely.

Makes about 5 dozen cookies

Peanut Butter Toffee Chewies

1 package (about 18 ounces) yellow cake mix with pudding in the mix
1 cup peanut butter
¼ cup (½ stick) butter or margarine, softened
¼ cup water
1 egg
1⅓ cup milk chocolate toffee bits, divided

1. Preheat oven to 350°F. Line cookie sheets with parchment paper.

2. Beat cake mix, peanut butter, butter, water and egg in large bowl with electric mixer at medium speed 1 minute or until well blended. Stir in 1 cup toffee bits.

3. Drop by rounded teaspoonfuls about 1½ inches apart onto prepared cookie sheets. Flatten tops of cookies slightly with back of teaspoon. Sprinkle remaining toffee bits into centers of cookies.

4. Bake 10 to 12 minutes or until edges are lightly browned. Cool 5 minutes on cookie sheets. Remove to wire rack; cool completely.

Makes about 4 dozen cookies

Heart Cookie Pops

1 package (about 18 ounces) strawberry or red velvet cake mix with
    pudding in the mix
½ cup butter, melted
2 eggs, lightly beaten
2 tablespoons honey
24 cookie sticks
    Prepared frosting
    Valentine candy decorations and sprinkles

1. Combine cake mix, butter, eggs and honey in large bowl until well blended.
Refrigerate dough 30 minutes.

2. Preheat oven to 375°F. Line cookie sheets with parchment paper.

3. Shape dough into 1-inch balls. Press 2 balls of dough together and taper
bottom to form point of heart. Place 2 inches apart onto prepared cookie sheets.
Place cookie stick under and halfway up each heart; press lightly. Repeat with
remaining dough and sticks.

4. Bake 10 to 12 minutes or until edges are light brown. Cool 3 minutes on
cookie sheets. Remove to wire rack; cool completely. Frost cookies; decorate
with candy and sprinkles.   *Makes 2 dozen cookie pops*

Orange Chai Spice Sandwich Cookies

1 package (about 18 ounces) orange cake mix
5 tablespoons butter, melted
2 eggs
1 tablespoon pumpkin pie spice
2 teaspoon ground ginger
1 teaspoon orange extract or vanilla
¼ cup cream cheese, softened
¼ cup prepared creamy vanilla frosting
½ cup orange marmalade

1. Preheat oven to 350°F. Spray cookie sheets lightly with nonstick cooking spray.

2. Combine cake mix, butter, eggs, pumpkin pie spice, ginger and orange extract in large bowl with electric mixer at low speed until well blended. Drop dough by rounded teaspoonfuls about 2 inches apart onto prepared cookie sheets.

3. Bake 10 to 12 minutes or until tops are puffed and cracked. Cool 5 minutes on cookie sheets. Remove cookies to wire racks; cool completely.

4. Beat cream cheese and frosting in small bowl until well blended. Stir in marmalade. Spread rounded teaspoonful of frosting mixture onto flat sides of half of cookies. Top with remaining halves.

Makes about 2 dozen sandwich cookies

Orange Chai Spice
Sandwich Cookies

Cinnamon Apple Pie Bars

1 package (about 18 ounces) spice cake mix with pudding in the mix
2 cups uncooked old-fashioned oats
½ teaspoon ground cinnamon
¾ cup (1½ sticks) cold butter or margarine, cut into pieces
1 egg
1 can (21 ounces) apple pie filling and topping

1. Preheat oven to 350°F. Spray 13×9-inch baking pan with nonstick cooking spray.

2. Combine cake mix, oats and cinnamon in large bowl. Cut in butter using pastry blender or fingers until butter is evenly distributed and no large pieces remain (mixture will be dry and have clumps). Stir in egg until well blended.

3. With damp hands, press about three-fourths mixture into bottom of prepared pan. Spread apple pie filling evenly over top. Crumble remaining dough over filling. Bake 25 to 30 minutes or until top and edges are lightly browned. Cool completely in pan on wire rack.   *Makes about 24 bars*

Tip To make handling easier, line the baking pan with foil, leaving a 2-inch overhang. When bars are cool, lift out of the pan using the overhang.

Pecan Coconut Layer Bars

Crust
- 1 package (about 18 ounces) yellow cake mix
- 5 tablespoons butter or margarine, melted
- 1 egg

Topping
- ¾ cup corn syrup
- ¼ cup packed brown sugar
- 2 eggs
- 1 teaspoon vanilla
- 1 cup chopped pecans
- ¾ cup sweetened flaked coconut

1. Preheat oven to 350°F. Line 13×9-inch pan with foil and spray lightly with cooking spray.

2. For crust, combine cake mix, butter and 1 egg in large bowl until well blended (batter will be stiff). Press batter into prepared pan; bake 15 minutes.

3. For topping, combine corn syrup, brown sugar, 2 eggs and vanilla in another large bowl until well blended. Stir in pecans and coconut. Spread mixture evenly over partially baked crust.

4. Bake 25 minutes or until top is bubbling and edges are lightly browned. Cool completely in pan on wire rack. *Makes about 24 bars*

Pumpkin Cheesecake Bars

1 (16-ounce) package pound cake mix
3 eggs, divided
2 tablespoons butter or margarine, melted
4 teaspoons pumpkin pie spice, divided
1 (8-ounce) package cream cheese, softened
1 (14-ounce) can EAGLE BRAND® Sweetened Condensed Milk
    (NOT evaporated milk)
1 (15-ounce) can pumpkin (2 cups)
½ teaspoon salt
1 cup chopped nuts

1. Preheat oven to 350°F. In large bowl, on low speed, combine cake mix, 1 egg, butter and 2 teaspoons pumpkin pie spice until crumbly. Press onto bottom of ungreased 15×10-inch jelly roll pan.

2. In large bowl, beat cream cheese until fluffy. Gradually beat in EAGLE BRAND® until smooth. Beat in remaining 2 eggs, pumpkin, remaining 2 teaspoons pumpkin pie spice and salt; mix well.

3. Pour into prepared crust; sprinkle with nuts.

4. Bake 30 to 35 minutes or until set. Cool. Chill. Cut into bars. Store leftovers covered in refrigerator.   *Makes 4 dozen bars*

Pumpkin Cheesecake Bars

Hanukkah Cookies

Cookies
   ¾ cup butter or margarine, softened
   2 egg yolks
   2 tablespoons grated orange peel
   1 package DUNCAN HINES® Moist Deluxe® White Cake Mix

Frosting
   1 container (16 ounces) DUNCAN HINES® Vanilla Frosting
   3 to 4 drops blue food coloring
   3 to 4 drops yellow food coloring

1. For cookies, combine butter, egg yolks and orange peel in large bowl. Beat at low speed with electric mixer until blended. Add cake mix gradually, beating until thoroughly blended. Form dough into ball. Cover with plastic wrap and refrigerate for 1 to 2 hours or until chilled but not firm.

2. Preheat oven to 375°F.

3. Roll dough to ⅛-inch thickness on lightly floured surface. Cut with Hanukkah cookie cutters. Place 2 inches apart on ungreased cookie sheets. Bake at 375°F for 6 to 7 minutes or until edges are light golden brown. Cool 1 minute on cookie sheets. Remove to cooling racks. Cool completely.

4. For frosting, tint ½ cup Vanilla Frosting with blue food coloring. Microwave at HIGH (100% power) for 5 to 10 seconds, if desired. Place writing tip in pastry bag. Fill with tinted frosting. Pipe outline pattern on cookies. Tint ½ cup frosting with yellow food coloring and leave ½ cup frosting untinted; decorate as desired. Allow frosting to set before storing cookies between layers of waxed paper in airtight container. *Makes 3½ to 4 dozen cookies*

Jingle Bells Ice Cream Sandwiches

1 package (about 18 ounces) devil's food cake mix
5 tablespoons butter or margarine, melted
3 eggs
50 hard peppermint candies, unwrapped
1 quart vanilla ice cream

1. Preheat oven to 350°F. Spray cookie sheets lightly with nonstick cooking spray.

2. Beat cake mix, butter and eggs in large bowl with electric mixer at medium speed 1 minute or until blended and smooth. Drop by rounded tablespoons 2 inches apart onto prepared cookie sheets. Bake 12 minutes or until edges are set and centers are no longer shiny. Cool 5 minutes on cookie sheet. Remove to wire rack; cool completely.

3. Place peppermint candies in medium resealable food storage bag. Seal bag; crush candies with rolling pin or back of small skillet. Place crushed candies in small bowl.

4. Line shallow pan with waxed paper. Place scoop of ice cream onto flat side of one cookie. Top with a second cookie; roll edge in crushed peppermints. Place on shallow pan. Repeat with remaining ice cream, cookies and peppermints. Cover pan; freeze until serving.

Makes about 1½ dozen sandwiches

Gingerbread Cookies

1 package (about 18 ounces) spice cake mix
½ cup all-purpose flour
2 teaspoons ground ginger
½ cup butter (1 stick), melted
⅓ cup molasses
1 egg, lightly beaten
Decorator icing and candies

1. Combine cake mix, flour and ginger in medium bowl. Beat in butter, molasses and egg with electric mixer at medium speed until combined. Place dough in resealable food storage bag and chill at least 4 hours.

2. Preheat oven to 375°F. Roll out dough on lightly floured surface to ¼-inch thickness. Cut cookies using 3- to 4- inch cookie cutters. Bake on ungreased cookie sheets 10 minutes or until edges are lightly browned. Cool 3 minutes on cookie sheets. Remove to wire racks; cool completely. Decorate with icing and candies. *Makes about 2 dozen cookies*

Festive Fudge Blossoms

¼ cup (½ stick) butter, softened
1 package (about 18 ounces) chocolate fudge cake mix
1 egg, lightly beaten
2 tablespoons water
¾ to 1 cup finely chopped walnuts
48 chocolate star candies

1. Preheat oven to 350°F. Cut butter into cake mix in large bowl until mixture is crumbly. Stir in egg and water until well blended.

2. Shape dough into ½-inch balls. Roll in walnuts; press gently to adhere. Place about 2 inches apart on ungreased cookie sheets.

3. Bake cookies 12 minutes or until puffed and nearly set. Place chocolate star in center of each cookie; bake 1 minute. Cool 2 minutes on cookie sheets. Remove to wire racks; cool completely. *Makes about 4 dozen cookies*

Cherry Cheesecake Bars

1 can (21 ounces) cherry pie filling or topping
2 tablespoons water
1 tablespoon cornstarch
1 package (about 18 ounces) cherry chip or yellow cake mix with pudding
    in the mix
½ cup (1 stick) butter or margarine, melted
1 egg
1 container (about 24 ounces) refrigerated ready-to-eat cheesecake filling

1. Place cherry pie filling in medium saucepan. Stir water and cornstarch together in small bowl until cornstarch is dissolved. Stir cornstarch mixture into pie filling until well blended. Cook and stir over medium heat until mixture comes to a boil. Boil 2 minutes, stirring constantly. Remove from heat; set aside to cool.

2. Preheat oven to 350°F. Spray 13×9-inch baking pan lightly with cooking spray.

3. Combine cake mix, butter and egg in medium bowl until well blended (mixture will be crumbly). Press mixture into bottom of prepared pan. Bake 15 minutes; set aside to cool.

4. Spread cheesecake filling evenly over cooled crust. Spread cooled cherry topping over cheesecake filling. Cover lightly with plastic wrap; refrigerate 4 to 24 hours before serving.   *Makes about 24 bars*

Cherry Cheesecake Bar

White Chocolate, Cranberry and Oatmeal Dippers

1 package (about 18 ounces) spice cake mix
1 cup old-fashioned oats
⅓ cup vegetable oil
2 eggs
1 teaspoon vanilla
1 cup dried cranberries
1 cup chopped walnuts or pecans (optional)
2½ cups white chocolate chips, divided
3 tablespoons vegetable shortening

1. Preheat oven to 350°F. Spray cookie sheets lightly with nonstick cooking spray.

2. Combine cake mix, oats, oil, eggs and vanilla in large bowl until well blended. Stir in cranberries, walnuts, if desired, and 1 cup white chocolate chips.

3. Drop by tablespoonfuls 2 inches apart onto prepared cookie sheets. Bake 10 minutes or until edges are lightly browned. Cool 5 minutes on cookie sheet. Remove to wire racks; cool completely.

4. Place remaining 1½ cups white chocolate chips and shortening in small microwavable bowl; heat on HIGH 15 seconds. Stir until mixture is melted and well blended. (Heat additional 10 seconds if needed).

5. Spread sheet of waxed paper on work surface. Dip each cookie into chocolate mixture and allow excess to drip into bowl. Place cookies on waxed paper; set aside until chocolate sets. *Makes about 1½ dozen cookies*

White Chocolate, Cranberry
and Oatmeal Dippers

Holiday Thumbprint Cookies

1 package (8 ounces) yellow cake mix
2 teaspoons grated orange peel
3 tablespoons orange juice
½ teaspoon vanilla
5 teaspoons strawberry fruit spread
2 tablespoons pecans, chopped

1. Preheat oven to 350°F. Spray cookie sheets with nonstick cooking spray.

2. Beat cake mix, orange peel, juice and vanilla in medium bowl with electric mixer at medium speed 2 minutes or until mixture is crumbly. Beat on medium-high speed 2 minutes or until smooth. (Dough will be very sticky.)

3. Coat hands with nonstick cooking spray. Shape dough into 1-inch balls. Place balls 2½ inches apart onto prepared cookie sheets. Press center of each ball with thumb. Fill each thumbprint with ¼ teaspoon fruit spread. Sprinkle with pecans.

4. Bake 8 to 9 minutes or until cookies are light golden brown and no longer shiny. Remove to wire racks; cool completely.   *Makes 20 cookies*

Tip   Although these cookies are called thumbprints, sometimes it's easier to use your index finger to make the indention.

Acknowledgments & Index

The publisher would like to thank the companies listed below for the use of their recipes in this publication.

Dole Food Company, Inc.

Duncan Hines® and Moist Deluxe® are registered trademarks of Pinnacle Foods Corp.

EAGLE BRAND®

The Hershey Company

©2009 Kraft Foods, KRAFT, KRAFT Hexagon Logo, PHILADELPHIA AND PHILADELPHIA Logo are registered trademarks of Kraft Foods Holdings, Inc. All rights reserved.

© Mars, Incorporated 2009

Metric Chart

METRIC CONVERSION CHART

VOLUME MEASUREMENTS (dry)

⅛ teaspoon = 0.5 mL
¼ teaspoon = 1 mL
½ teaspoon = 2 mL
¾ teaspoon = 4 mL
1 teaspoon = 5 mL
1 tablespoon = 15 mL
2 tablespoons = 30 mL
¼ cup = 60 mL
⅓ cup = 75 mL
½ cup = 125 mL
⅔ cup = 150 mL
¾ cup = 175 mL
1 cup = 250 mL
2 cups = 1 pint = 500 mL
3 cups = 750 mL
4 cups = 1 quart = 1 L

VOLUME MEASUREMENTS (fluid)

1 fluid ounce (2 tablespoons) = 30 mL
4 fluid ounces (½ cup) = 125 mL
8 fluid ounces (1 cup) = 250 mL
12 fluid ounces (1½ cups) = 375 mL
16 fluid ounces (2 cups) = 500 mL

WEIGHTS (mass)

½ ounce = 15 g
1 ounce = 30 g
3 ounces = 90 g
4 ounces = 120 g
8 ounces = 225 g
10 ounces = 285 g
12 ounces = 360 g
16 ounces = 1 pound = 450 g

DIMENSIONS

1/16 inch = 2 mm
⅛ inch = 3 mm
¼ inch = 6 mm
½ inch = 1.5 cm
¾ inch = 2 cm
1 inch = 2.5 cm

OVEN TEMPERATURES

250°F = 120°C
275°F = 140°C
300°F = 150°C
325°F = 160°C
350°F = 180°C
375°F = 190°C
400°F = 200°C
425°F = 220°C
450°F = 230°C

BAKING PAN SIZES

Utensil	Size in Inches/Quarts	Metric Volume	Size in Centimeters
Baking or Cake Pan (square or rectangular)	8×8×2	2 L	20×20×5
	9×9×2	2.5 L	23×23×5
	12×8×2	3 L	30×20×5
	13×9×2	3.5 L	33×23×5
Loaf Pan	8×4×3	1.5 L	20×10×7
	9×5×3	2 L	23×13×7
Round Layer Cake Pan	8×1½	1.2 L	20×4
	9×1½	1.5 L	23×4
Pie Plate	8×1¼	750 mL	20×3
	9×1¼	1 L	23×3
Baking Dish or Casserole	1 quart	1 L	—
	1½ quart	1.5 L	—
	2 quart	2 L	—